INSIDE THE TANK

- a memoir of four years in
Margaret Thatcher's Prime Minister's
Policy Unit 1986-1990

By George Guise

First Published 2015
Text Copyright © George Guise 2015
George Guise asserts his moral rights to be recognised as the author of this work.

Bretwalda Books, Unit 8, Fir Tree Close, Epsom, Surrey KT17 3LD
info@BretwaldaBooks.com
www.BretwaldaBooks.com
ISBN 978-1-910440-08-7

Printed and bound in Great Britain by
Marston Book Services Ltd, Oxfordshire

Contents

FOREWORD

No headhunter recruited George Guise from Consolidated Gold Fields to Margaret Thatcher's Policy Unit at No.10 and that was just one of many reasons why he was an inspired choice.

George gives us a fascinating insight of how the "Gestapo" of the Policy Unit drove the privatisation programme that so defined the Thatcher years.

Not long before George came to Downing Street, Harold MacMillan, enobled as the Earl of Stockton, spoke in the House of Lords accusing the Conservative Government of Margaret Thatcher of "selling the family silver". It is amazing to think today that critics of her drive to move so much of British industry from the public to private sector were not only found in the Labour Party.

Margaret Thatcher was convinced that free entreprise would make a better job of running British businesses than the dead hand of the state. But George had to remind her that entrepreneurs may talk about how they welcome competition but secretly they dream of private monopolies.

George reveals much of the less recognised side of Margaret Thatcher the scientist and the deep interest she expressed in research and the rewards for intellectual property.

George Guise's experience in the mining industry brought invaluable practical experience to Margaret Thatcher's Policy Unit, he is one of the unsung heroes who played a central role in the Thatcher revolution that weaned so much of Britain off taxpayer funding and made us proud nation again."

Lord Hamilton of Epsom

PREFACE

In the Spring of 1986, I had dinner with Brian Griffiths, the then Head of the Prime Minister's Policy Unit and I described the endless battles between our head office in London and the American, Australian and South African businesses of the Consolidated Gold Field Group of which I was an executive director. The only thing upon which the overseas businesses agreed was common enmity towards the London Headquarters. Brian said that it was the same thing in Government, a perpetual battle between the spending Departments and The treasury with No 10 Downing St as the referee !

Ten days later, I was invited to visit No 10 in order to meet the other members of the PM's Policy Unit - seven impressive individuals ranging from the recently retired senior partner of a leading accounting firm to the seconded head of strategy from Shell. Shortly thereafter, I was invited to join too in order to advise the PM on commercial and industrial matters, particularly privatisation. This brief was soon expanded to cover science policy, the arts, and even to a limited extent South Africa, as set out later.

The speed with which this happened may have been in part due to my also being Chairman of The Royal Philharmonic society, where one of the trustees was Robert Armstrong, the extremely charismatic and likeable head of the Civil Service. There was a natural antipathy between the Policy Unit and the established Civil Service, so perhaps there was hope that I might help to heal the rift. If so, they were wrong.

I had never met Margaret Thatcher and shortly after I joined the Unit in September, I was waiting, somewhat tensely, outside her study in order to brief her on some matter. It was a Thursday evening and she came scurrying back late from the House of Commons. "Oh, Mr Guise, I am so sorry to be late. Do go into the study and pour yourself a drink - I do hope you drink !" Soon afterwards, when I was settled with a large gin and tonic, she asked me what I knew of the European Commission and I replied "Very little".

"Well, I shall tell you," she began with relish. "It is like membership of a club where Britain and Germany pay in a pound and get 60 pence back and are told exactly how to spend it. The other members pay in less than 60 pence, get back more than a pound and spend it exactly as they choose!"

The Policy Unit under Thatcher derived from Harold Wilson's "kitchen cabinet" headed by Marcia Williams rather than Heath's Central Policy Review Staff which operated under Victor Rothschild. We received copies of everything the PM received, other than defence and foreign policy documents, and had the opportunity of commenting in writing before the PM saw them.

Each PU member had a special area of advice and normally attended meetings with the PM. This frequently included the relevant spending minister as well as the Chancellor. My own areas initially covered commercial and industrial matters but later expanded to cover other areas including science policy where I found MT heavily at odds with the mood in Whitehall which was that expenditure on scientific research should be targeted on utilitarian goals. She held a strong personal belief in the value of basic curiosity driven research but had few allies among ministers or officials.

When she discovered that I had read physics at Oxford, held a research degree, and maintained a strong interest in basic science, she asked me to review all the science material sent to her and advise. This was both exciting and daunting as she was no mean scientist herself. Indeed, she held a chemistry degree and had done research on the saponification of glycerides which led to the invention of Mr Whippy ice cream in the fifties.

I also had the opportunity of advising her on matters involving the Arts and, to a limited extent, South Africa. These were areas where I had some specific knowledge or involvement and MT was always interested in views from people who knew what they were talking about. What she deplored was lobbying on behalf of vested interests which merely repeated other people's opinions without adding any new knowledge.

This account focuses on matters where I had detailed personal involvement with MT. I do not digress into second hand views and opinions. There has been an abundance of such things published since her death, some indeed by those who never even met her !

PRIVATISATION FROM 1986

The Sale of the Rover Group to BAe was the first major issue upon which I advised the PM. This didn't happen until 1988 although I became involved from 1986 when I was shown the financial plan for the company under continued state ownership. This was highly reminiscent of the endless pleadings we received from loss making Gold Fields operations. More money required before we can make profits!

The DTI were clearly in the pockets of Rover and fully supported every crazy proposal from the Rover management. There was a perpetual fear that the Chairman would resign unless Rover got its way on everything. The Chairman, a bearded Canadian with a business academic background, had a good record at British Shipbuilders, which was essentially an unrelated group of mainly loss making shipyards, many of which he rightly closed. This had gained him a high reputation with MT, which was generally known, and allowed him to ride roughshod over DTI officials.

My Gold Fields career had made me wise to this kind of individual, several of whom we had fired in order to get the Australian and American operations right. I was resolute in the belief that once the shareholder became subservient to management, all strategic direction was lost and and with it any hope of returning to profitability. The mantra from Rover which the DTI was afraid to challenge was that Rover could only be saved by more injection of Government money.

There were already huge borrowings approaching £2bn which the 1987 and 1988 plan proposed to increase. I argued that it was pointless building more cars which no one wanted to buy - the Rover market share had been dwindling for several years and by 1987 had halved to

15% over 15 years. When it was suggested that other, cash conserving, plans should be considered, DTI officials cowered, fearing that the Chairman would resign.

For years, it was the received wisdom from Rover and the DTI that interest payments were killing Rover and the figures, as presented in the various annual plans, made it difficult to verify or falsify this contention. So in February 1988, I set out, with help from the Treasury, to recast the annual plan and demonstrate to MT that it was not interest but Rover's own capital expenditure plans which were destroying the company. Even if the borrowings were cancelled, as Rover frequently urged upon HMG, the company was still hemorrhaging cash and no one in his right mind would buy the business and follow the 1988 plan as presented to HMG.

Once MT was convinced that the 1988 business plan could never lead to either a trade sale or a placement, events moved swiftly. The plan was rejected and Rover realised that the game was up as far as MT was concerned. Having told us that there was no prospect of privatising Rover without spending a fortune developing more new models, they announced a sale to British Aerospace within weeks. We were told that this was a piece of serendipity out of the blue but later evidence suggests that secret talks had been taking place with BAe for some time.

Clearly a very different business plan for Rover would be followed under BAe's ownership. Only Archie Hamilton, then in the political office at No 10, showed prophetic concern that ownership of Rover might ultimately destroy British Aerospace which very nearly happened some years later.

To much Whitehall rejoicing the details of the sale were announced, the Government guaranteed borrowings would be cancelled and BAe would pay some £300m for the assets. However the European Commission, although having agreed to the cancellation of the HMG guaranteed debt, were still proving sticky about the terms of the sale, asking ever more questions of the DTI about details of closing and completion. The DTI tried to poo poo all this saying that the Commission were being tiresome as ever, a line with which MT was normally sympathetic. Not this time! MT glanced sharply at the senior DTI minister present saying that she hoped that we were being honest with the Commission. It subsequently turned out not to be so.

Despite the many tiresome parts of the Commission, the Competition Directorate DG4 is an unqualified force for good, and indeed it was they who had spotted an 11 month delay between closing, when all terms are irrevocably agreed between parties, and completion, when payment is made by the buyer to the seller. As the assets being transferred were valued at £300m and ambient interest rates were 11%, this was an illegal state aid of £33m. HMG was subsequently fined for this deception by Brussels during the Major Govt. The Treasury claimed not to have spotted this, suggesting that it was a private agreement between Rover and BAe timed exactly to fit within a single public expenditure year and therefore be invisible in the public accounts.

The story at Jaguar was very different. In 1980 this state owned company was restructured and isolated from British Leyland as a separate entity, Jaguar Cars Ltd, with its own management. It was eventually privatised in 1984. Annual production had risen from 14 000 cars in 1980 with annual productivity of 1.2 cars per employee to 50 000 cars by 1988 with productivity of 4.5 cars per employee, which compared with Mercedes at 5.5. It had also established a professional worldwide sales and distribution network with 60 per cent of sales in the USA. The chairman, John Egan, regularly appeared on the factory floor and knew many of the employees on christian name terms.

It was therefore little wonder that there was much interest, especially from Ford, in buying the business. However, the company was protected from foreign takeover by a "golden or special share" held by the Trade Secretary which was due to expire in 1991. Ford was lobbying for this to be annulled early.

By October 1988 the pressure had grown to the point where Jaguar came to the PM with a bizarre scheme which was effectively a takeover proofing device. The company would be restructured with three strategic shareholders, each holding 20% including a foreign manufacturer such as Ford, and the Hong Kong and Japanese Jaguar distributors. The balance would be split among existing shareholders, employees and a placement. This scheme was presented as a guarantee of Jaguar's independence for a further seven years. It was argued that the principal competitors, Mercedes, BMW and Porsche had such takeover protection in Germany.

Having come from the mining industry, which was infested with takeover protection schemes, I was dead against this which was in flagrant breach of the Takeover Panel's code and sought to lock out private shareholders from any control over management who claimed that neither the unions nor the share market understood the business. MT soundly rejected it !

Sometime afterwards, as the special share was approaching expiry, the UK chairman of Ford telephoned me one Friday afternoon, while the share market was still open, to tell me that Ford intended to bid for Jaguar as soon as the market closed. He thought that "the Lady would like to know". I told him that was the last thing she wanted to know and that, mercifully, she was at her Finchley constituency. However, he had effectively imprisoned me in my office, away from the telephone until the market closed. The Jaguar share price shot up 50% that weekend.

Ford thus became the owner of Jaguar whose fortunes have blossomed ever since.

By contrast, the fate of Rover under the ownership, and wholly ineffective "management", of HMG is an object lesson in the utter folly of the state trying to own and operate a commercial business.

British Shipbuilders and Harland and Wolff ran a close second. In the late eighties there was massive over capacity in the world's major shipyards. The main civilian yards in the UK were North East Shipyards in Sunderland and Govan in Scotland, both part of British Shipbuilders (BSL) falling under the DTI. Whereas the Northern Ireland office was responsible for Harlands in Belfast.

In 1987 the build cost for a standard 30 000 ton bulk freighter in the UK was around $25m compared with $23m in Germany or Japan and only $14m in South Korea. The average world price for a carrier of this size was some $13m so even South Korea was building ships at a loss. Despite the hardening of the Yen and the Deutschmark during the eighties, the UK was still at the top of the world cost curve.

Both Harlands and BSL argued for continued intervention funds to keep the yards open with massive subsidies promised to potential customers such as China. The "strategic" case was always that of Mr Micawber, that there was "bound" to be an upturn in the market. Indeed, the market had historically shown a doubling between peaks and troughs, but, even if this eventually happened again, the UK yards would never make up the cash hemorrhage required to keep them open.

BSL was draining the taxpayer of £70m per annum whereas closure costs were estimated at £220m for both yards together. The comparable closure figure for Harlands was given as £300m which no one believed because their estimates were notoriously unreliable. It was said that Harlands couldn't build a galvanised bath tub within 100% of estimate! MT had to be restrained from quoting this wisecrack in front of the Harland Chairman, John Parker.

The case for closure or distressed sale was overwhelming and both the DTI and the Northern Ireland Office accepted this. The Scottish Office was more reluctant and kept arguing that Govan had a long term future, evidencing some interest in the yard from Norway. The procrastination and pious hope from the Scottish Office contrasted with Northern Ireland because the cost of keeping Govan open came not from the Scottish budget but from the DTI. In the case of Harlands, the money had to be found from the NI budget!

MT decided to bang heads because she wanted to announce a total plan for all three yards. The British Shipbuilders Act of 1983 required BSL to privatise or close its remaining assets and this was eventually achieved with Govan being sold to the Norwegian firm Kvaener later in 1988. All other BSL activities ceased in 1989. Today, Govan is owned by BAe Systems and builds warships for the Royal Navy, currently the two unnecessary and unaffordable aircraft carriers ordered by the Brown Administration.

HMG sold Harland and Wolff in 1989 to the Norwegian shipping tycoon Fred Olsen in partnership with a management buyout. After completing some LPG carriers, it ceased shipbuilding, in favour of heavy engineering design work such as bridges. Today it is mainly involved in offshore renewables and a cynic might therefore say that it is still bleeding the taxpayer!

After the hopelessness of Rover and Shipbuilding, whose business plans were identical:

"More government money please in order to lose more money", as MT put it, dealing with the privatisation of **British Steel** was a pleasure. Under a succession of excellent chairman, especially Ian MacGregor appointed in 1980, BSC had doubled productivity from 13 man hours per tonne of liquid steel to 6.2 by 1987, whilst a trading loss in 1981 of £500m had become a profit of £200m. The main factor was a ruthless reduction in manning from 200 000 to 50 000 over the same period.

This achievement was against an overcapacity of 100 million tons worldwide. Furthermore, BSC had five integrated steel plants scattered all over the country, Llanwern and Port Talbot in Wales, Ravenscraig in Scotland, and Teesside and Scunthorpe in England. BSC managed this overcapacity of some 30 percent adroitly. Because integrated plants are so capital intensive, with a very high fixed cost element, they must run continuously which leads to pressure to sell the surplus at any price which contributes to fixed costs. Clearly, the successful steel companies of the future would tend to have manufacturing concentrated at a single site.

Such considerations led BSC to propose closing Ravenscraig in the run up to privatisation which was scheduled by the end of 1988. Strip steel production would be at Port Talbot and Llanwern while general steels would be located at Teesside and Scunthorpe. Closing Ravenscraig would add over £100m to BSC's annual profit which, because the higher earnings would thus become more secure, would have a double effect on BSC's value as a public company. Barclays, who were the advisers to BSC, reckoned that, with Ravenscraig closed, overall value would be over £2bn but, with it open, this would fall to below £1.3bn.

Needless to say, this provoked hostility from the Scottish office who wanted to keep Ravenscraig open even at the cost of a weaker and less valuable BSC privatisation. The eventual compromise was to close the hotstrip mill, with a loss of 700 jobs, but to continue steelmaking with Ravenscraig producing semi finished products for shipment to LLanwern while the latter was installing continuous casters. One ridiculous suggestion, soundly trounced by MT, was that the articles of association of the newly floated BSC should contain a clause that there would always be steelmaking in Scotland!

Among the other crazy suggestions from the Scottish office was to delay BSC privatisation while the possibility of floating a separate Scottish steel company was examined. MT replied that this was the worst of all courses. While BSC was under one ownership, the 30 per cent overcapacity in strip steel could be accommodated. Were a separate business to be made from the Ravenscraig/Dalzell complex, the consequence would be cut-throat pricing to the point where both businesses lost money.

Ironically, it was MT herself who had to be converted to this point of view. When I first entered the debate in late 1986, she told me that she was firmly of the view that BSC should be broken up and not privatised as a monopoly. People had been getting at her about the mistakes in the privatisations of British Telecom and British Gas which had been sold as monopolies, before my time at No 10. She said that she did not wish to repeat this with Steel.

I argued that BSC was not a monopoly, even if its management might wish it were, because a third of BSC's output was exported while a third of UK consumption was imported. As I had much experience of the US steel industry, whilst at Cons Gold Fields, I went to America to gain a view from those heads of the steel companies whom I knew.

I was back within a week and even before I had time to pen a report, she stopped me in the corridor. "Well, what do your American friends say?" I replied that they agreed with her, that BSC should be broken up. She paused for quite a while and then said, "That means that I am wrong if that's what the competition want".

BSC was successfully privatised in late 1988 as a single entity and after merging with a Dutch company became Corus Group in 1999. In turn, this was bought by Tata in 2007.

The long saga of **electricity privatisation** began in the autumn of 1987 with a day long meeting at Chequers which I attended and at which MT presided. It included the newly appointed Energy Secretary, Cecil Parkinson, along with senior officials from the Treasury, DTI, and other interested departments. The purpose was to agree a structure for the privatisation of the CEGB, then chaired by Walter Marshall who was not present.

The broad structure agreed was that 12 regional electricity distribution companies (RECs) would be formed which would jointly own the National Grid (NGC). These would carry the obligation to supply electricity in their areas. There would be only two Electricity generation companies, National Power (NP), which would contain both fossil fuelled and the nuclear generators and be chaired by Walter Marshall.

The second smaller company, Powergen (PG), would contain only fossil fuelled generators and be chaired by Bob Malpas, recently of BP. The generating companies would not carry any obligation to supply and would compete with each other to provided power into the grid. An electricity "pool" would be set up where NP and PG would bid into the pool offering prices (the pool input price) depending on the volume called for by the RECs. The pool output price would then be settled as the price which equalised supply and demand. Bids would be entered and cleared every twenty four hours.

There was some criticism of this arrangement, not least from MT, because this would set up a supply duopoly from the outset. However, the argument prevailed that NP had to be big enough to contain the nuclear plants, which had to operate fully or not at all to provide a base load for NP. Furthermore, the RECs had full freedom to source their supply outside the duopoly from new entrants or even build their own generators. In this way, it was believed that the duopoly would ultimately wither as new electricity sources came on line.

It was also agreed that these newly privatised companies should be protected from takeover by the creation of a special or "golden" share which the Energy Secretary would retain. It would carry no dividend or management rights unless a takeover bid appeared when it would immediately carry sufficient votes to block acceptance of the bid. In the case of the RECs, the special share would have a limited life of five years. However, in case of NP and PG, some argued for a perpetual share, especially the Scottish office on the spurious grounds of national security. Although this was strongly opposed by the Treasury and the DTI, MT did not force the issue which went unresolved.

My own advice, which was eventually taken by MT, was that short term takeover proofing was reasonable, while management got to grips with the realities of operating in a truly commercial world. However, permanent protection of management from the wishes of its shareholders could only lead to growing inefficiency and ultimate decline. I had seen much of this in the mining industry during my previous existence at Consolidated Gold Fields. The argument based on National security was especially weak. In an emergency government can take control of any strategic asset, as the present government points out in encouraging investment in new British nuclear plant by France and China.

In the summer of 1989 there came a bombshell from the Dept of Energy. The figures which we were given at Chequers for nuclear decommissioning were hopelessly wrong. These now totalled £4bn plus £1bn for Scotland. Such a figure on the balance sheet of NP would make it insolvent and therefore unfloatable. Inevitably, the DEn's solution was an injection of £4bn of special equity prior to flotation. The alternative was to exclude the nuclear plants from the flotation. Either course left the

Government in a mess. Such a large injection of taxpayer funding would put NP into the Rover category of a distressed sale of a national disaster.

It was therefore decided to exclude the nuclear plants from the sale. This led to the resignation of Walter Marshall, who had constantly argued for a completely risk free privatisation of NP with guaranteed future profitability. All cost overruns, whether from decommissioning, impositions by the Nuclear Installations Inspectorate, or incompetent management, to be met by the taxpayer. Even though MT admired Marshall, she agreed that this was no way to privatise anything, with or without nuclear. Trevor Holdsworth was subsequently appointed chairman of a non nuclear NP and privatisation planning proceeded.

MT was clearly peeved that we had to exclude the nuclear plants from NP. So it was fortunate that a chance soon came to re-establish her nuclear credentials. This was the decision in mid 1990 to proceed with the construction of the second pressurised water reactor, Sizewell B. What many did not realise was that there was a financial case for continuing even though the return on capital from nuclear plant was poor once decommissioning was taken into account.

Of the £2bn total cost of Sizewell B, £1bn had already been spent so the avoidable cost was only £1bn. This meant that electricity needed to be sold at only 2.6 pence per kWh which was less than the 3.5 pence from a new coal station. Of course, to make a viable return on the total cost would require an electricity price of 5 pence which would have been completely uncompetitive.

"This Government has not lost its faith in nuclear power just because bad initial advice from your department led us to believe that NP's antediluvian reactors were sellable." was MT's fiery response to one hapless official who suggested that a positive decision on Sizewell B could demonstrate governmental inconsistency.

Now that nuclear had been removed from the privatisation, some of us tried to revive the original case for a further split into four or five generating companies and so greatly improve competition from the outset. MT's phrase was " We have built a large enough cage to contain the nuclear bear but now there is now no bear in it". However the timetable was against this course because the plans for the RECs, which were to own the grid, were well advanced. The nightmare was that a general election might fall between the privatisation of the RECs and the Power companies.

As if all this wasn't enough, the PG management started to play up about the cost of installing flue gas desulphurisation (FGD). The DEn, advised by Kleinworts, valued PG at £1.6bn, anticipating a recovery in electricity wholesale prices after 1994, whereas PG, advised by Warburgs who did not anticipate such price recovery, valued the company at only £1.1bn. In addition, PG wanted a cash injection from HMG of £400m prior to flotation in order to cover future costs of FGD. This would have reduced net proceeds from the flotation to a mere £700m. PG were expecting the taxpayer to sell 20GW of installed generating capacity, one third of the UK total, for the capital cost of building 2GW.

Their position was outrageous and the DEn, now led by John Wakeham, and with MT's full support, decided to get tough. They went behind Powergen's back in order to test the possibility of a trade sale - ie no flotation - and one very successful British company showed considerable interest. Although negotiations never got to a final figure, the vicinity of £1.6 bn, Kleinwort's valuation, was clearly in the right ballpark. Once Powergen were made aware of this, their position collapsed and successful privatisation, without any FGD injection, proceeded along with the rest of the electricity industry.

With hindsight, there are several lessons to be learnt, many of which apply to the current debate about energy prices. First, it was a terrible mistake to allow generators to acquire RECs and thence to muddy the separation of the obligation to supply. Secondly, NGC should have been left under the ownership of the RECs. The decision to allow it to merge with the gas supplier, Centrica, opened the door to cross subsidisation of gas and electricity leading to opacity in true costs and prices.

Thirdly, HMG's decision to load energy bills with "green levies" for uneconomic windmills etc and subsidies for poor households, has further distorted the energy market. If an elected government wish to impose such things, they should find the funds centrally, not load captive electricity and gas customers. Thatcher would never have done it. At the time of writing, the Cameron government has belatedly recognised this.

Airbus was never a true candidate for privatisation because our european partners, France (avionics and final assembly at Toulouse), Germany (fuselage) and Spain (tail) were in the project for the "gloire" in facing up to American manufacturers Boeing and Mcdonnell-Douglas. British Aerospace made the wings and was continually at HMG for subsidy, which they called "Launch Aid" to insulate them from losses, arguing that this was what the partner countries' governments did. MT supported the Airbus venture but wanted to see it become profitable, rather than an exercise in "keeping up with the Jones's" - her regular riposte when wheedling ministers wanted to waste taxpayers' money because other countries did.

Launch aid was established in the sixties to help the British aircraft industry over a limited period while a successful market presence was established. However BAe regarded itself as the custom builder of airbus wings on behalf of HMG. It saw itself simply as an agent of the DTI and claimed to have no influence over pricing.

MT argued the exact opposite, that BAe, through its membership of the Airbus Industrie management board, should force through structural and pricing policy changes which would lead to profitability. It would only do this if forced to shoulder the full financial responsibility of being a participant. If this failed then it should withdraw from the venture.

In 1988 BAe argued that participation in the A330 and A340 large passenger aircraft programs would lead to losses of near £4bn by the year 2000. They "manufactured" this number by making the most negative assumptions about exchange rates, prices, volumes, and costs. When challenged, it was clear that no sensitivity tests had been made on these key parameters and MT thought it outrageous that they should come to HMG for a handout without such crucial financial calculations available.

We had made it very clear that any further financial launch aid for BAe would be treated totally separately from the Rover sale which was subject to an impending British Aerospace AGM. However, there were dark hints that failure to secure the former could jeopardise the latter, although MT never believed this because BAe were getting such a fantastic deal on Rover - £1bn of assets for a net payment of £150m.

The most that HMG conceded was that if the European Commission reduced the net contribution from HMG to BAe, viz £650m then the reduction would be given to BAe in the form of Launch Aid for Airbus. This meant that the total cash contribution from HMG would remain at £650m which, of course excluded the huge debt write off totalling £2Bn.

The other great obstacle to privatising Airbus was its very structure as a "Grouping of Economic Interests" (GEI) rather than a PLC. This was a very uneasy partnership of confused objectives, the French, Germans and Spanish being primarily political, whilst the British ever since Thatcher's ascendency, was profitability. The management arrangements were hopeless with the overbearing President of Bavaria, Franz-Joseph Strauss, as chairman of the supervisory board and politicians everywhere. There was no finance director at board level and the only nexus of financial responsibility was one vice president of seven reporting to the general manager.

It was clear that the only way forward was to persuade Strauss to step down so that a proper management structure could be installed and MT bravely volunteered to try to do this at a small Downing St meeting in July 1988. However, the cat got out of the bag at a DTI breakfast meeting the same day with the predictable response "If mine ears hear this they will shout until the windows will shake!" Later, MT assured me that her windows were quite intact. Herr Strauss died two months later on October 1st while hunting.

In 2001 a joint stock company was formed with an amalgamation of the continental european interests, EADS, holding 80 percent and BAe's successor, BAE Systems, holding 20 percent. In 2006, this stake was sold to EADS, with Britain finally disentangled from Airbus. However, Launch Aid continued spasmodically until it was finally condemned by the World Trade Organisation in June 2010.

There were several other privatisations in the pipeline when MT was ousted by the hubris of a failed politician at the end of 1990. Many of these came to term under John Major's subsequent ministry with varying success.

In April 1989, HMG announced the abolition of the **Dock Labour Scheme** (DLS), which was a heinous restrictive practice begun in 1947 and reinforced by the supine Heath Government in 1972. It gave dockers a job for life, however badly they performed, and made it a criminal offence to employ anyone not sanctioned by the Transport and General Workers Union (TGWU). Inevitably, the performance of British ports deteriorated being plagued with endless strikes.

Four months of strikes followed this announcement ending in a legal battle with, predictably, the House of Lords supporting the dockers. We were tackling several other restrictive practices at the time (doctors, teachers, barristers, even judges) and MT was quite fearful of a rerun of the 1984 miners' strike. But Jack Jones was no Scargill. MT soldiered on and the scheme was finally abolished in July, with a defeated labour force returning to work.

In short order, strike free British ports became competitive leading to a return of much international transshipping which had been lost to northern europe. This led to proposals to privatise the Trust Ports, beginning with Tees and Hartlepool. Trust Ports had been created by incompetent Labour legislation in 1966 which never even defined the ports' ownership - cf the Trust Bank. Furthermore, as the Wilson Government had never envisaged the possibility of the ports becoming profitable, cash surpluses were trapped inside the port authority and could not legally be spent on anything other than the area of the port. This lunacy led MT to comment that it would be perfectly legal to gold plate every crane within the port but not to build a container warehouse immediately outside.

The privatisation of Tees and Hartlepool, via a private member's bill, was nearly lost because of the interference of the Treasury who tried to grab half the proceeds of sale for the exchequer. There was no legal justification for this and such an amendment would have meant that the bill would become hybrid and therefore lost in that session of parliament. So HMT was put firmly back in its box and the Tees and Hartlepool bill was passed in March 1990.

This experience showed that it would be a parliamentary shambles to leave the remainder of the Trust Ports to privatisation via private bills. So the Ports Act was conceived in order to give HMG the power to force trust port privatisation and was eventually enacted by the Major Government in 1991. Four more trust ports were subsequently privatised, Clyde, Forth, Medway and Tilbury. There was then a long lull until the return of the Cameron Government in 2010 with its great need for cash.

Coal and Rail were done badly with the centralisers and monopolists back in control. For example, the logical way to privatise coal was to sell each pit to its proximate power station, the transfer price of the coal would then be an internal matter with competition manifest in the electricity market. Admittedly, this would have made better economics if MT had been able to float four or five generating companies rather than just two.

What actually happened was that after the closure of the most hopeless mines, a grouping of the remainder was offered for sale as a single entity. Several buyers showed interest and the Treasury opted for the highest price which came from an over optimistic Richard Budge. This meant that the new coal company was overloaded with debt and, as many of us predicted, it was back within a few years, asking for government handouts.

With rail, it was a great mistake to leave the track company, Railtrack, in separate ownership from the Train Operating Companies (TOCs). This meant that whenever an accident happened, Railtrack and the relevant

TOC briefed lawyers and entered into months of argument about who was responsible. In addition, Railtrack rolled out a never ending capital program which they tried to finance by overcharging the TOCs for track use. This muddled arrangement was clearly unstable and government had to re-enter, regulating prices and generally being led up the garden by the railway engineers. This has left Britain with the most expensive railway system in the world.

A far better plan would have been to use the electricity privatisation model with the TOCs jointly owning the track. After all, why should the movement of electrons around the country follow different economics from transporting people?

We also had fledgling privatisation plans for the **Post Office** of which only Girobank came to fruition although the DTI (rather grandly renamed the Board of Trade) did come forward with a half baked scheme which the Major government threw out. It is very much to the present government's credit that in 2013, more than 20 years later the Post Office is finally out of HMG's ownership.

The rest of Northern Ireland's state owned industry was in the same situation as Harland and Wollf. Massive losses with the continual plea for more state money in order to lose more money. The biggest spenders were James Mackie & Sons (Mackies), a textile machinery manufacturer and foundry in West Belfast and the aircraft and missile manufacturer, Short Bros (Shorts). Mackies, once the largest employer in NI, had gorged taxpayers' money for decades and eventually closed in 1999 after a series of crippling strikes.

Shorts was even worse, with the chairman in open rebellion against the government, and arguing that the company would only become economically viable if the state injected money to develop new aircraft - about £400m was sought in 1988 to design and build the FJX. This was very reminiscent of Rover's pleading and MT was having none of it even though Northern Ireland Industry regularly claimed that it was a special case because of the "troubles".

The Treasury, normally a staunch ally against wasteful spending, actually argued for putting money into Shorts in early 1989 because it had a £600m surplus which it wanted to hide! This would have had the Shorts management laughing all the way to the bank and devising ever more wasteful schemes for the next Public Expenditure Round.

MT said No!

The missile business was potentially viable but bedevilled by the refusal of the Shorts management to separate it from the hopeless aircraft business, even though the two had nothing in common and even operated from different sites. Eventually, Shorts was bought by Bombadier Aerospace of Canada in 1989 and, as a specialist manufacturer of aircraft components, has thrived to become the largest manufacturer in Northern Ireland. This shows what can be achieved by a tough management team, which is not beholden to the state.

Electricity Privatisation in Northern Ireland had a major reversal of strategy in mid 1990. It had been generally assumed, including by MT, that the whole business was too small to benefit from introducing competition and that this would actually increase costs and electricity prices.

The advising banks were strongly against any break up or separation of generation from supply, arguing that the minimum size to achieve efficient production and distribution was more important than forcing out monopoly profits. Only the Treasury gave strong support to Northern Ireland ministers for splitting the electricity business, pointing out that reduced proceeds, because of the elimination of monopoly profits, was in the national interest!

Eventually MT became convinced that introducing competition would not necessarily impose any net cost. It was eventually agreed that privatisation would be via a flotation of the distribution and supply business and trade sales of the generators. This was not popular with the trade unions or Northern Ireland Electricity (NIE) which MT regarded as evidence that the right decision had been made !

EVENTS IN THE CITY OF LONDON

1986, when I joined the Policy Unit, was a time of enormous activity and change in the City. £13 bn was spent on acquisitions and mergers compared with £7bn the previous year and only £1bn in 1981. Deregulation and the abolition of fixed commissions had vastly increased the pressure on financial institutions to promote takeover activity with promoters regularly proposing low return targets and even arranging the necessary finance, a practice forbidden in the USA by the Glass Steagall Act which Clinton foolishly repealed leading to the banking havoc of 2008.

In 1986, the fledgling Securities Investment Board (SIB) with the nested Self Regulatory Organisations (SROs) within it had only recently been invented and the demarcation between it and non regulatory institutions, such as the Takeover Panel of the Stock exchange, was still under debate. The Panel was under increasing criticism for ineffectiveness and inconsistency and, with 14 full members all drawn from City institutions, operated much like the committee of a gentleman's club. Its protagonists championed self regulation, arguing that the law is clumsy with the policing of the Companies Act left to heavy handed DTI officials and the Fraud Squad. Whereas the Panel had all the subtle "insight" and authority to identify and kick out "wrong uns".

This might have worked well when stock market behaviour could be left to a caucus of honourable gentlemen whose financial circumstances left them immune to temptation and greed. MT could see that the world had evolved otherwise with the Panel having lost much respect. There was a new generation of "red braces" operators who had grown up with the philosophy that if you knew something was going to be more expensive in the afternoon, then you bought it in the morning!

The abolition of fixed commissions and the huge pressure for increased stock exchange throughput led to widespread takeover talk, proposals for greenmail, white knighting and indeed anything which led to greater transaction volume. This is exactly what happened in New York in the 70s after the abolition of fixed commissions and MT and her ministers were under great pressure to act. The problem was that no one knew what to do! MT herself naturally believed in deregulation but, like most of her ministers, was naive about the consequences of a "free for all".

Compared with Washington, where anyone within hailing distance of the White House or the Capitol, had probably made several million and knew SEC and FTC regulations inside out, UK ministers were amazingly ignorant of, for example, the difference between a Class 1 and Class 2 transaction, disclosure requirements, or the acceptance requirements for a takeover. The UK had competition authorities in the form of the Office for Fair Trading (OFT), and the Monopolies and Mergers Commission (MMC), now called the Competition Commission. The Trade Secretary had the power to block a merger or takeover if the MMC found that it was against the national interest but not otherwise.

The definition of National Interest had become extremely vague and so in 1984, Norman Tebbit defined it very narrowly in competition terms, implying that market share and therefore the protection of consumers, should be the fundamental criterion addressed by the MMC. MT had a very rosy view of competition, believing that the great businessmen of the day exalted it. I eventually won a great argument with her, pointing out that entrepreneurs hated competition and would do everything they could to get around it. She only latterly came to the view that business success was bound to breed monopoly, as it had with 19th century capitalism, unless Government prevented it.

The forces at work in the City had led to highly leveraged bids, financed for example by junk bonds, which could leave the predator so highly borrowed that it had to sell many assets of the victim company as well as stopping all expenditure such as research which did not produce immediate profit. The DTI was very reluctant to identify very high leverage as a matter for the MMC to investigate if there was no competition issue and this matter continues to vex the Government and the Bank of England today. The recent proposals from Pfizer to acquire Astra Zeneca generated a wave of hostility in Britain with the Trade Secretary having no power to prevent it unless so advised by the Competition Commission.

This is nothing new. In 1986, the bid by BTR, one of Britains most successful companies, for Pilkington Glass had stirred a hornet's nest of protest, not least from the unions and the incumbent management who were united against the bid. The ASTMS union (now part of Unite) made a submission to the OFT which stated "We do not believe that BTR have made a case for being allowed to take over Pilkington". For its part, the Pilkington Management doubled its profit forecast to £250m for 1987! In the Pilkington case there were neither competition nor high leverage concerns.

The hostile bid had become the norm in Britain precisely because shareholders had relegated the fate of their business to management boards, selling out their shareholding if they didn't like the way the business was managed. Without effective external involvement at board level as in America or Europe, the first sign that directors have been found wanting is the appearance of a hostile bid ! The management's gut reaction is to run to the competition authorities for protection even when there is no competition issue which is a profound misuse of a government procedure.

MT was certainly aware of these issues and her instinct was to leave well alone and let the market decide. However there were occasions where a false market had developed through insider trading or price manipulation or both. Indeed Guiness probably went to the "wrong" bidder, Distillers, because of this, even though some of the key players were eventually prosecuted following action by the DTI.

My own old company, Consolidated Gold Fields, was subject to the largest takeover bid in British history from the South African Anglo American group in 1988 and in this case the Govt did refer the bid to the MMC although the argument on competition grounds was thin. It was clear that a false capital market had developed in the company's shares which should have been enough grounds to delay the bid.

However, under the Tebbit guidelines, the only sure way was to develop an argument based on competition in the international mineral sands market. The bid was therefore delayed and, because of a combination of Panel rules and American judicial procedures, the bid lapsed. But it was close run. Eventually, the company was bought and dismembered by the Hanson Group who almost certainly overpaid.

The confusion about City Policy was never truly resolved under the Thatcher premiership and has continued to this day with various ineffective policing proposals. The Financial Services Authority under Labour effectively emasculated the Bank of England and proved so ineffective that one wag likened it to mice trying to control cats!

SCIENCE POLICY

MT frequently argued that individuals, not structures, achieve. It therefore took some convincing her that research expenditure by Government was in an unholy mess largely because the Harold Wilson mentality about "the white heat of technology " had grown deep roots,especially at the DTI and the Research Councils. The chairman of the Advisory Council on Science and Technology (ACOST), Francis Tombs, was also chairman of Rolls-Royce and the Government's Chief Scientist was John Fairclough from IBM. Moreover, Arnold Weinstock of GEC was always lobbying for ever more spending on the likes of Nimrod, the air defence system he was building despite the availability of AWAC, an "off the shelf " system from America.

No senior civil servant had any science education beyond O level and those Government officials with a scientific background were corralled into "the scientific civil service "under a departmental chief scientist who generally lobbied for the interests of his department. In any case, his comments in cabinet papers were often relegated to the tenth appendix or beyond, even when the issue was of critical national scientific importance such as membership of CERN (see later) or participation in other joint international science programs.

During the early nineteen eighties there was a general Whitehall attitude that too many crazy people were building radio telescopes or atom smashers and that a Thatcherite administration should focus research on utilitarian goals. This is exactly the recently declared policy of the Canadian Government and the opposite of MT's personal view which was instinctively suspicious of industry oriented programs.

Against the very vociferous lobbying of industry, especially manufacturing and defence, she became convinced that top industrial management rarely values research for which it has not paid. I showed her examples such as Dunlop seeking research funds for carbon fibre golf club shafts and one instance where an academic had convinced the DTI that it should support his research into better adhesives for the soles of shoes. We compared the sorry state of our electronics and aerospace industries, which had gorged state funds since the war, with the pharmaceutical and chemical industries which had not and flourished.

I helped her tackle this issue during 1987 with some very detailed analysis which demonstrated that industry was siphoning off funds from the total tax funded research budget and that, although the overall spend was comparable with other leading economies, basic research was being increasingly starved. She acted decisively and took over the chairmanship of a cabinet committee previously chaired by the Chancellor and renamed it so its remit was crystal clear, Committee for Science and Technology. Its first meeting took place on July 1st 1987.

MEMBERSHIP OF CERN

At MT's behest I visited CERN near Geneva in May 1987, the first of many visits over the years. She was concerned that various independent reports had indicated excessive cost overruns and poor financial controls. There were even some voices suggesting that the whole enterprise was a colossal waste of money because no economic benefit would ever come out of it (Get thee to Ottawa!).

I reported my overall impression that great work was being done in a field where Britain had excelled over the years and that a great number of very impressive British scientists were at work there, both in the theory division (eg John Ellis) and on accelerator design (John Bell - also renowned for work on fundamental quantum theory). The then Director General was Herwig Schopper, later succeeded by Carlo Rubbia, who had earlier won the Nobel for identifying the W and Z bosons predicted by Abdus Salam (see later) and others.

Schopper was acutely aware that the administrative system and financial controls were inadequate and explained that the Cern management is very restricted in what it can change without the agreement of all the then membership of 14 different countries. When Cern was set up in the 1950s, powerful ministers sat on the council but over the years the administration had become increasingly fossilized forcing the management to grind on with antiquated procedures.

My essential advice to MT was that Britain should definitely not leave Cern but that it should increasingly force improved administration. She took the argument that Britain should not be forced out of a field, particle physics, which it had led for centuries because of poor administration.

Over the next year, the UK's position largely prevailed, thanks, inter alia, to Chris LLewellyn Smith at Oxford, later to become Director General of Cern, who devised a mechanism for recalculating the British sterling contribution.He was also particularly helpful in providing MT with many examples of where basic science had led to enormous economic benefits. Also the then CERN Director, Carlo Rubbia, realised that he would have to implement stringent cost control if he wanted to free himself for proper scientific planning and management. The Large Electron-Positron Collider (LEP) tunnel was well advanced and the Large Hadron Collider (LHC)was already a gleam in his eye!

At this time it was MT's belief that the USA would never abandon the Texas based 87km Hadron Collider and join Cern instead. She died owing me a £10 bet!

I rejoice that MT's view about Cern prevailed over some of her myopic colleagues. It would have been invidious not to be a member of the collaboration which has so recently found the Higgs boson, an event which will adorn the history of science.

CLIMATE CHANGE AND THE ROYAL SOCIETY SPEECH OF SEPTEMBER 27TH 1988

In July 1988 MT told me that she was planning to give a speech to the Royal Society, of which she had been elected a Fellow, and asked me to help her write it. My initial idea was to trumpet the basic shift in government funding from applied to basic science and indeed this remains a key ingredient of the final speech.

However, she was advised by Charles Powell, Crispin Tickell, James Goldsmith and others that this represented a key opportunity to express concern at what might be happening to global climate, a matter which had not seemed to concern MT unduly hitherto. However, the wily politician realised that this matter was brewing in the depths of the UN, where Tickell was the UK representative. So far the only head of government, Gro Brundtland, the socialist PM of Sweden, had shown concern with her advocacy of a policy of "sustainable development". Thatcher, both through genuine concern and political opportunism, decided to trump her.

The major theme of the Royal Society speech, certainly the one upon which the world wide press focussed, was that " we (may) have unwittingly begun a massive experiment with the system of this planet itself ". Every major morning headline carried variations on "The Maggon goes Green". Thatcher had shot Brundtland's fox!

For the rest of her administration, the green theme continued. However MT was worried that the subsequent hysteria would lead to over prescriptive actions against industry before the science was adequately understood. Her own position, as I continually advised, was to make adequate funding available so that governments could establish what exactly was going on. For this reason she did support the establishment of the Intergovernmental Panel on Climate Change

(IPCC) and wanted to see it adequately funded.

On ozone depletion, and the reduced use of chlorofluorocarbons in refrigeration and aerosols, she was a great champion and willingly signed up to the Montreal protocols in 1988.

On global warming, then called the greenhouse effect, she was much more cautious fearing the self infliction of economic damage on prosperous economies would encourage the anti- industrial left, then licking its wounds from the world wide implosion of communism. She fully recognised that this was a field where opinion far outweighed both study and ideas. She never argued for inaction but called for more data collection and computer modelling, especially on the behaviour of the oceans and sea level rises. John Houghton of the Meteorological office was particularly helpful.

Economic solutions, such as James Goldsmith's proposal that a market be created in which Third World debt could be traded, used to advantage the fact that a majority of threatened rain forests were in third world countries with debt problems. There were also similar proposals that international aid would be dependent on forestry conservation. Although MT supported much of this and held conferences to further such ideas, the Foreign Office were implacably opposed to linking foreign aid with the recipient governments' environmental behaviour. Unfortunately, she was swept from office before such nonsense could be demolished.

COMMERCIAL EXPLOITATION OF BRITISH INNOVATION

MT was very critical of Britain's failure to exploit discoveries made here, only to see foreign companies reap great commercial benefit. Her favourite examples were the failure to patent liquid crystal displays, initially developed by GEC under an MoD contract, and the failure of the Laboratory for Molecular Biology (LMB) at Cambridge to capitalise on the large scale production mechanism for monoclonal antibodies which had won Cesar Milstein the Nobel prize in 1984. Her argument was that Britain might lead the world in science but that our scientists were woefully naive in foreseeing the commercial benefits.

I decided to investigate this argument, which was also prevalent at the DTI, with their endless "innovation" and "enabling technology" programs, frequently an excuse for taxpayer funding of near market research. I visited the LMB and met Aaron Klug, its then director, Cesar Milstein and Francis Crick, who was visiting from the USA, all landmark figures in breakthrough science. These were certainly not commercially naive people. Indeed, Milstein reminded me of the wily steel dealers I had encountered in America, of whom it was said "They could make money in a phone booth".

What had actually happened in the Milstein case was that he was very well aware of the enormous commercial benefit which his process could bring and wanted the LMB to take out a patent. However, the Treasury would not allow this because "it had not been budgeted". Milstein offered to take out a patent at his own expense but was told that he couldn't because the intellectual property was not his as it had been funded by HMG. Meanwhile, time was running because he could be pipped at the post for the Nobel if he did not publish soon. In the event he did, received the Nobel prize and watched as the pharmaceutical industry in the USA made billions from his work.

The story at GEC was similar. I learned that GEC had begged the MoD to take a commercial patent on the liquid crystal technology which it had developed under a secret HMG contract for cockpit displays in fighter aircraft. This was refused and GEC had the frustrating experience of watching the Japanese rediscover LCDs and install them in millions of wristwatches throughout the seventies and eighties.

MT was appalled and herself pointed out that Nimrod might have been a successful air defence system if the Treasury had not insisted that it be developed using spare comet aircraft which were due to be scrapped and were, anyway, too small to accommodate the extensive electronic equipment which Nimrod required.

Edicts issued forth from No 10 that henceforth, organisations like the LMB, which were administered by the research councils, should be encouraged to exploit their research and reinvest a large part of the proceeds. In this way, the scanning tunnelling microscope, then under development at the LMB, has led to commercial exploitation greatly to that organisation's benefit.

Sometimes it was the other way around. In the late eighties, Alec Jeffreys at ICI developed a DNA probe which could identify microscopic human samples with near 100 percent accuracy. This rightly interested the Home Office which was in negotiation with ICI for a royalty based licence to use the probe. However, ICI was playing tough on price so the Home Office tried to get MT's support for sequestering the device using a process known as Crown Right. The argument was that this was in the national interest because serial killers and rapists could be identified quickly before they could do further harm.

No 10 was sympathetic to the enforced use of the probe in urgent cases involving life or death, as indeed was ICI. However the Home Office wanted the penny and the bun and tried to sequester general use of the probe, for example, in identifying relatives of immigrants. No said MT, for that they have to pay ICI a commercially negotiated price.

The use of the DNA probe is a political hot potato today with Jeffreys and the Govt trying to scale back the storage of an individual's data by a recalcitrant police force.

DEPARTMENTAL RESEARCH PROGRAMS

The exception to MT's broad policy of taxpayer funding of basic work, where the science was not understood, while leaving applied work intended to generate profit to the private shareholder, was the development work which enabled Govt departments to fulfil their own remit.

In these fields, as everywhere else, there was endemic confusion between value for money, return on capital, and the boundaries between research, development and procurement. Of course, vested industrial interests exploited this to get as much from the taxpayer as possible.

The Policy Unit did not brief on Defence per se but did become involved with defence procurement, on projects including the European Fighter Aircraft (EFA), the next generation of tanks (Abrams versus Challenger) and, as mentioned previously, the choice between Nimrod and AWAC airborne defence. There was always a marked proclivity towards developing a British or European system, if necessary from scratch, rather than acquire American equipment off the shelf. This often leads to a misstatement of defence research costs versus procurement because the prototype equipment, upon which large research funds have been spent, normally itself goes into service.

The self sufficiency argument is understandable but it did, and still does, lead to enormous waste and bloated overrunning budgets. It sometimes leads to major political spats, with very long term consequences, such as the 1986 resignation of Michael Heseltine from the Cabinet. MT decided to support the American company Sikorsky's purchase of the British Westland Helicopter Company, as advocated by the Westland board, rather than back a costly and uncertain European rescue as favoured by Heseltine.

One of the DTI's pet projects was the British National Space Centre (BNSC) which, when reduced to its elements, was a national strategy for "keeping up with the Joneses" as MT put it. British Aerospace was keen to retain the status quo which enabled it to syphon off taxpayer funds for projects which would give "economic competitive advantage to the UK". Apart from wanting more money, up to £30m per annum from 1990, there was a suggestion that the BNSC should be a freestanding cost centre within Whitehall outside the DTI. This would have set it up, like the UK Atomic Energy Authority (UKAEA), to become one of Government's big spenders. Fortunately, MT nipped the idea in the bud. "They are attempting to build a pulpit for industrial lobbyists!"

MT belief was that space investment should not be part of the science budget at all because the means for establishing equipment in space was well understood and the future should therefore be technological effort driven by commercial rationale. It was only after these financial runaway proposals were rejected by HMG that industry was pushed into directly financing space activity.

BNSC, and its associated industry pressure groups, had been completely captivated by French arguments for grandiose "man in space" projects rather than bolstering successful achievements such as communications satellites and remote sensing.

These arguments prevailed and by mid 1989 BNSC had ceased to embarrass the Government by lobbying for huge expenditure and had settled into an interdepartmental coordinating role. It was pushing for greater industrial funding of space applications and, as Britain's representative at the European Space Agency, had efficiently renegotiated our participation in the polar platform project - a surveillance system which orbited the earth from north to south and therefore covered the entire earth's surface every 24 hours.

The Energy department was heavily engaged in developing the next generation of nuclear reactors.

The Prototype Fast Breeder Reactor (PFBR) had been operating on the north Scottish coast for several years and by the middle of 1988 was producing 250 MW of electricity into the Scottish Grid. This is a tiny amount, more nuisance value than commercial value, despite the taxpayer having contributed £3.5 bn up until then. Annual operating costs in 1988 were over £100 m compared with the £12m received for electricity generated !

The rationale for developing the FBR program in the nineteen sixties was that the price of enriched uranium was predicted to soar. So that a device which made its own fuel, by generating fissile plutonium from natural uranium, seemed like a winner. However, it was a massive commercial failure only capable of operating with vast taxpayer subsidy and, as Thatcher pointed out, a classical example of Government folly in trying to pick winners using very long term economic criteria. A similar mistake is being made today with the wind farm program.

The UKAE tried to argue that the PFBR was not a commercial project and that research should continue on fuel reprocessing as well as the overall fuel cycle.When all else failed, the prospect of unemployment in Caithness was advanced. To my surprise, MT was remarkably sympathetic to this case. She had visited Dounreay, liked the community, but recognised that the FBR operation had to terminate.

She asked about the possibility of continuing research on the fuel cycle under commercial contracts or equity participation from countries which still favoured a breeder reactor program such as France or Japan. This had clearly never been considered by the UKAEA, which had operated as a hopelessly uncommercial arm of the Energy Department with an unfortunately large measure of independence. Indeed, it was the Government's electricity privatisation program, with its emphasis on profitability, which heralded the death knell of the UKAEA.

The other great civil nuclear research project was a mega European collaboration, the Joint European Torus (JET) being constructed at Culham near Oxford. This was absurdly long term; in 1990 a commercial fusion reactor was promised by the year 2060. This was a classic example of the top down, finance driven approach which often fails to solve practical problems.

Nevertheless, I argued that we had a very different situation from the PFBR. Whatever, the economic follies of the past, the decision of the Wilson Government to act as host for JET had left Culham with the most sophisticated magnetic torus machine in the world. It had been a great scientific success in finding out how plasmas behave at very high energy and that even the most intractable problem of the plasma's interaction with the vessel's wall was beginning to be solved.

We did not therefore support the Treasury's proposal to switch off JET before its research program had been completed. The scientific case for extending the program until 1996 was good but so was the economic case, because the torus had already been built. The most productive fusion reaction for energy generation is that between the two heavy isotopes of hydrogen : deuterium and tritium. All the work hitherto had been leading to the introduction of tritium into the reactor chamber and this was proposed within two years, in 1990.

To stop the project before introducing tritium would have been like abandoning a bridge when it was within reach of the other side of the river. MT was taken with this argument but also agreed that the funding arrangements on the British side had been naive to the point of farce. We were paying a 10 percent "host country premium". Decommissioning costs, as always, had spiralled and the economic case for a fusion reactor, as for a fast breeder, had weakened.

It was therefore agreed to complete the research program at JET, provided Britain ceased to pay any host country premium after 1990 and that the European partners be pressed to help with decommissioning. It was also argued that Britain should not participate in the Next European Torus (NET) but favoured an extended international project, involving the USA, Japan and Russia,the International Thermonuclear Experimental Reactor (ITER).

By 1986 Agriculture was absorbing annually over £120m, namely 13% of all civil departments research spending, and this excluded the £50m spent by the Agricultural and Food Research Council (AFRC).

The industry had, and still has, an overall return on capital well below the national cost of capital and government was expected to make good the balance. It was therefore no wonder that taxpayer funded R&D spending had so mushroomed! A vicious circle existed whereby more research led to more overproduction leading to more subsidies. Curbing this was difficult because of the European Common Agricultural Policy (CAP) with the French Government, as ever, in the pockets of its farmers.

Nevertheless, MT was determined to try and prune the government financed research budget of this prima donna among industries.

The principle argument from the Ministry of Agriculture, Fisheries and Food (MAFF) was that agriculture, and particularly horticulture, is composed of a large number of small firms who cannot afford a research program. The starting premise is that someone must fund near market research otherwise British farmers and horticulturalists would be unable to compete, especially with European producers receiving massive government grants. The logic then goes on to support the imposition of blanket levies on large producers in order to fund R&D for the entire industry. Any shortfall was inevitably picked up by HMG.

The Agricultural Development and Advisory Service (ADAS), the organisation within MAFF which conducted this work, employed half of its staff. MT's attitude was to privatise any successful parts of ADAS and close down the rest. "This Government was not elected to grow flowers !" ADAS subsequently became an executive agency of MAFF and was eventually privatised in 1997.

We never felt that the curtailment of MAFF's near market research programs had been as successful as in other fields, largely because European Commission (EC) programs and protocols had largely usurped Britain's ability to act independently. The Common Agricultural and Fisheries Policy continues to bedevil British interests today.

The Dept of transport had a smaller annual research budget at £25m and spent much time trying to reconcile the EC's vehicle emission limits with lean burn technology and the use of three way catalysts as (unsurprisingly) advocated by Johnson-Matthey who made them ! No 10 had very little involvement with the transport research budget which was under reasonably tight control throughout the Thatcher period.

In the spring of 1989, Departments were asked for initiatives about global climate leading to a broadly based conference at No 10 which MT had agreed to chair. The contribution from the Dept of Transport was utterly defeatist seeking to capitalise on the perceived problem of CO_2 emissions in order to excuse their own failing transport policies. Their basic solution was vast increases in taxation on private transport to fund massive subsidies on public transport. This went right against the Thatcherite principles of consumer choice and dissemination of central control. " Doesn't sound much of a vote catcher" said she!

NOBEL PRIZEWINNERS LUNCH & VISIT OF ABDUS SALAM

In order to emphasise her support for basic science, MT held a lunch at No 10 in April 1989 for UK Nobel scientific prize winners, including foreign citizens who had conducted their work in Britain. Invitees included Cesar Milstein (Argentina) and Abdus Salam (Pakistan), neither of whom would take British citizenship because it would remove a Third World Nobel laureate. This meant that Abdus Salam could not use his knighthood in the UK. Ill health prevented him from attending the lunch, but see later..

The guests included Aaron Klug (1982 for development of electron microscopy), Godfrey Hounsfield (1979 for computer assisted tomography), Anthony Hewish (1974 for the discovery of pulsars), Frederick Sanger (1958 for the structure of insulin), Max Perutz (1962 for the structure of other proteins), Dorothy Hodgkin, MT's former tutor at Oxford, (1964 for the development of protein crystallography), George Porter (1967 for work on free radicals), Nevill Mott (1977 for the electronic structure of disordered systems), Brian Josephson (1973 for predicting macroscopic quantum phenomena), Andrew Huxley (1963 for excitation of the nerve cell membrane), Cesar Milstein (1984 for monoclonal antibody production - see earlier), James Black (1988 for Beta blockers), Geoffrey Wilkinson (1973 for the discovery of organometallic compounds), Peter Mitchell (1978 for ionisation in biological systems), and John Vane (1982 for work on prostaglandins). Most of these laureates held titles, either national or academic, which have not been included above.

Because the majority of attendees, which included Kenneth Baker, then Secretary for Education and Science, John Fairclough, the Govt Chief Scientist, and myself, were from outside Government, we were able to lay on a lavish lunch. MT sat alongside Dorothy Hodgkin, who suffered from severe arthritis, and helped her cut up her food. I had never seen the PM behave so deferentially to anyone as she did that day to her former tutor.

The lunch was deemed a great success and went a long way towards re establishing MT's credentials among scientists, Oxford having refused her an honorary doctorate several years earlier. Nevertheless, as we went up the staircase to her study afterwards, she commented to me " So much brain power concentrated in one room and all they wanted to talk about was money!"

I have mentioned that Abdus Salam had not been able to join us that day but we were able to arrange for him to visit MT in May and I had the great privilege of both briefing her for his visit and attending the meeting at which only the three of us were present. The meeting lasted at least an hour and began with a present from him in the form of a magnificent silken rug, woven in Pakistan. MT immediately rolled up and threw out the moth-eaten one in front of her mantelpiece and replaced it with Salam's present!

The conversation was wide ranging, from spontaneous symmetry breaking and the electroweak interaction to ideas about the development of research in the third world of which Salam was a champion. He told us about his Institute for Theoretical Physics in Trieste which he invited me to visit, and I did later that summer.

Towards the end of the meeting, he mentioned that he was seeing Benazir Bhutto, then Prime Minister of Pakistan, later that week. Our scientific conversation immediately ceased and was replaced by a set of instructions on how that country should be run! As so often happened with MT, the political opportunity was never missed.

ARTS POLICY

In October 1989 a vast document, longer than King Lear, arrived on my desk. This was the Wilding Report, an analysis by a retired senior civil servant of how the Arts Council operated and whether it required reform. For some reason, perhaps because she knew that I held the pro bono chairmanship of the Royal Philharmonic Society, the second largest concert giving society in the world after the Leipzig Gewandhaus, MT wanted my advice.

The report began with a laborious diagnosis of a straightforward problem, namely that the Regional Arts Associations were out of control, having been hijacked by local authorities while centrally funded by the Arts Council. The report did identify potential savings on bureaucracy and recommended the abolition of a separate "Crafts Council" which MT supported. "Basket weaving in the Cotswolds" was her caustic comment !

At the beginning of the year 1989 Peter Palumbo had taken up the chairmanship of the Arts Council and was a breath of fresh air, spending £50 000 of his own money on refurbishing the premises. His great initiative was to think up ways of increasing the ratio of private money which Britain spent on the arts, pointing out that in America it was 80%. His target, which I argued was too low, was a £50m fund raised privately. The Treasury took a dim view of initiatives such as tax deductibility or matching HMG funding and MT believed that, as the country was transformed back into wealth - by then we had a Treasury surplus - private giving would increase automatically. Unfortunately, there was a large element of pious hope in this belief !

The fundamental mindset which we were trying to confront was the long held Whitehall view that cultural activity was the government's rather than the citizen's responsibility. During the Labour period, when punitive taxation had driven enterprising people away and the nation into economic sloth, there was no alternative to total government funding of the Arts. Otherwise, Britain would have become as second rate culturally as it had economically. As many individuals and corporations were now prospering, MT and Palumbo, were attempting to make cultural giving fashionable as it was in America. This initiative was only partially successful but did achieve some impressive financial gestures from rich individuals such as the enormous support the Royal Opera House received from the South African Donnie Gordon.

At this time, 1988/9, the government was led to believe that the famous Thyssen collection of renaissance paintings, which the Thyssen Trust had decided to relocate from Lake Lugano to either Britain or Madrid, might become available. MT argued that, if this was indeed the case, Britain should act fast because using the Treasury surplus in this way would enhance the capital stock of Britain. We believed that we could acquire £600m of assets for little more than £200m.

Unfortunately, despite the apparent willingness of MT and Baron Thyssen, the trust of which he was chairman, was under the control of his Spanish wife and the collection went to Madrid.

SOUTH AFRICA

My background in the South African mining industry meant that I had many friends there and, indeed, used to spend the Christmas and New Year period in the Cape which gave me considerable insight into what was happening politically. I became friendly with our new ambassador there, Robin Renwick, who was very helpful in setting up meetings during my annual visits.

Although the Policy Unit did not normally brief on foreign policy, I did send MT reports between 1987 and 1990 on what I perceived to be the developing situation.She told me much later that she found these far more helpful than the regular Foreign Office briefs which, while falling short of actually recommending sanctions, kept pointing out how Britain was becoming increasingly "isolated" from those countries and organisations which did.

My general advice was that imposing trade sanctions was about the stupidest thing that could be done and might even lead to civil war. The poor whites were becoming increasingly desperate while the black and coloured workers on the fruit farms and the mines would face massive unemployment. This argument did not deter the great revolutionary leaders, safely ensconced in Hampstead or Lusaka, from leading the call.

The lie which the left was peddling was that apartheid was a manifestation of capitalism whereas it was in fact racial socialism designed to protect the low achievers at the bottom of the white population. MT was made well aware that the principle voices for reform were the successful capitalist organisations like Anglo American and the Rupert Group. Mercifully she became deaf to the increasingly vociferous clamour for sanctions, especially from those who knew nothing about South Africa and had never been there!

Ronald Reagan was a natural ally against sanctions but was more at the mercy of the "bien pensants" of congress who generally knew nothing of South Africa. One senator even suggested that, when I was next in SA, I should look up a friend of his in Nairobi "one weekend."

Although I have no direct evidence, it is my belief that MT dissuaded Reagan from the usual US foreign policy initiative of "Leap before you look"!

EPILOGUE
- OVERVIEW OF THATCHER'S STYLE

MT's operating method derived from her personality, not her philosophy of Government. The latter was both simple and, in the context of the seventies, revolutionary. Put at its crudest, it was to get the State's dead hand off as much national activity as possible. This included intervention in industry, centralised economic planning and, above all, the redistribution of income and wealth through taxation.

By contrast, her operating methods were highly interventionist, frequently involving second guessing Departmental proposals, driven by an innate suspicion that her ministers were being bamboozled by a recalcitrant Whitehall which she believed was fundamentally statist and averse to returning powers to individual citizens.

This inconsistency led directly to the success of her early ministries. The whole ship of state was so centralist, so corporatist, and enthralled by the belief that only large committees of "important personages" could achieve anything. A fussy, energetic and determinedly anti-statist bossy-boots poking her nose in everywhere was essential. The conventional Heath method of leaving the implementation of policy to ministers would never have generated the enormous upheaval and release of individual initiative which actually happened. Her Policy Unit was used as a kind of Gestapo to ensure that ministers were doing their jobs! Not always a comfortable position for the likes of myself.

I don't believe that MT really thought of herself as part of the Government but rather as someone whom the electorate had appointed to stop the Govt screwing up. At the beginning, before I joined the PU, she had a group of ministers, the Wets, who didn't believe that most of the

1979 Manifesto's promises could be achieved. They went.

By 1986, when I joined, she had a Cabinet largely of implementers who had formed good relationships with their officials but who were terrified of "thinking out of the box" although she claimed that was exactly what she wanted! Instances of new idea generation became increasingly rare unless someone at No 10, often the PU or the Private Office, had "tested it out with herself". Thus the Cabinet was no longer a decision making body but rather an executive carrying out the policies of one individual.

Domestic policies which were perceived to be Thatcherite were pursued regardless of national relevance and often in the face of open hostility, eg water privatisation, the community charge, the Bar legislation, fine details within the Health program. The Govt was widely perceived to have reneged on its own market philosophy by intervening in the foreign exchange market to the ultimate detriment of the exchange rate, interest rates and inflation. A remarkable hat trick!

There were too many timid, failed faces in the Cabinet who believed themselves to be blazing a Thatcherite trail but who were in fact isolating her from both party and electorate. Rhodes Boyson had a brilliant solution to the hardships of the Community Charge by transferring education costs from councils to the Treasury but was never allowed to put it to her. "We don't want the PM to get into one of her states!"

Her greatest weakness, which finally led to the disaster and which sprang from the noblest motive, was to value loyalty above competence.